The Story of
Hanukkah

Susanna Davidson

Illustrated by
Gianluca Garofalo

Reading consultant: Alison Kelly
Roehampton University

Contents

Chapter 1
The Jewish people

Hanukkah is a festival celebrated by Jewish people. Long, long ago, the Jews were shepherds and farmers, living in an area now known as the Middle East.

3

The Jews were one of the first people to worship one God. They believe their God gave them a set of laws to live by, known as the Ten Commandments.

The Ten Commandments

I am the Lord your God who saved you from slavery in Egypt. Worship no other God but me.

Do not make statues of other gods and worship them.

Always say my name with respect.

Work for six days and keep the seventh as a holy day of rest.

Respect your mother and father.

Do not murder.

Husbands and wives must be faithful to each other.

Do not steal.

Do not tell lies.

Do not be envious of other people's things.

Throughout the year, Jews celebrate different festivals. Each one has a story behind it...

The festival of Passover remembers the Jews' journey across the desert, when they fled from a life of slavery in Egypt.

Sukkot recalls when the Jewish people lived in the wilderness for forty years.

Purim is a festival to celebrate the day the Jewish Queen, Esther, persuaded the Persian king to save her people.

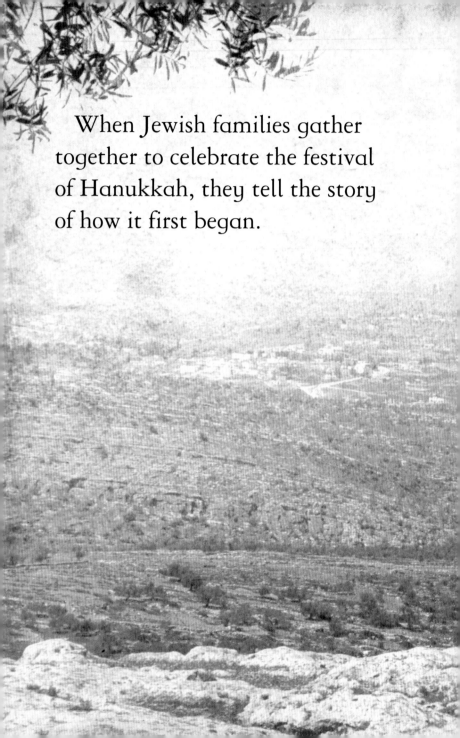

When Jewish families gather
together to celebrate the festival
of Hanukkah, they tell the story
of how it first began.

A view of the hills in Modin, Israel, where the Hanukkah story took place.

Chapter 2

A wicked king

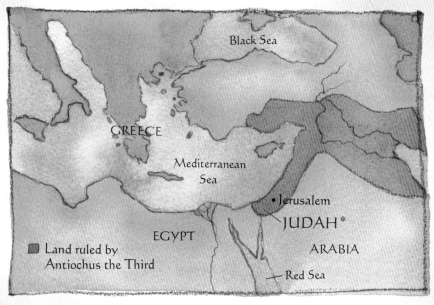

Black Sea

GREECE

Mediterranean
Sea

EGYPT

■ Land ruled by
Antiochus the Third

• Jerusalem

JUDAH*

ARABIA

— Red Sea

* Judah is now known as Israel.

Over 2,000 years ago, the Jews
settled in a tiny country called
Judah, in the Middle East. But they
didn't rule their own land.

Instead, their king was a powerful Greek, called Antiochus the Third, who was head of a huge empire. He let the Jews live in peace and keep their traditions.

On festival days, Jews came from far and wide to their holiest place of all...

...the Temple, in Jerusalem,
which stood on the top of a hill.
The Temple gates blazed with gold.

Inside was a courtyard, where Jews gathered together to give offerings of fruit, olives and wheat. One by one, they placed their offerings at the temple altar.

Then, led by the high priest, they said their prayers in Hebrew – the language of the Jews.

12

Beyond the courtyard, in a holy
room, stood a huge oil lamp, the
menorah. Only the purest oil was
used to keep the flames alight –
made from the first drop of oil from
each olive that was pressed.

But the Jewish people's lives were
about to change forever.

The old king died and his son, Antiochus the Fourth, came to the throne. He demanded that everyone worship Greek gods – including the Jews.

I'm banning Jewish festivals, Jewish books...

Then he passed a new law. "Jews must give up their religion... or die!" he declared.

Antiochus ordered his men
to march into Jerusalem. They
smashed up the Temple furniture
and stole the gold and silver.

They put up statues of Greek gods
in the Temple, as well as statues of
the king himself. Finally, they
burned the Jews' holy books.

"Now I shall send an army across the countryside," Antiochus decided, "and Jews everywhere will obey my laws."

Chapter 3

The fight begins

One hot summer's day, a group of
Antiochus's soldiers marched into
a sleepy village called Modin.

17

The soldiers rounded up the
villagers from the fields.

"From now on, you must all
worship the statue of this Greek
god," an officer ordered.

The villagers looked
at him in horror. The officer turned
to the leader of the village, an old
priest called Mattathias.

18

Around him stood his five sons – John, Simeon, Judah, Eleazar and Jonathan.

The officer thought if he could get Mattathias to obey him, everyone else would follow.

But Mattathias had fled from Antiochus's laws in Jerusalem. He wasn't going to put up with his orders again.

We'll reward you with gold.

"We will not obey the king's commands," he said. "We're not giving up our religion."

"If you don't, we have orders to kill you," replied the officer.

At that moment, a terrified villager stumbled forward, ready to worship the statue.

21

Mattathias rushed after the villager, his dagger drawn, and toppled the statue. Before the king's men could react, Mattathias's sons leaped to attack them.

After the bloody fight was over, Mattathias called his sons and followers together. "We must go to the hills!" he cried. "Our fight for freedom has begun!"

Chapter 4

The Maccabees

Over the next few months,
Mattathias and his men stayed
in the hills, learning how to fight
like soldiers. At night they crept
down to villages to gather
more support.

But life in the hills was harsh.
After a year, Mattathias fell
gravely ill. As he lay dying,
he gave a last message to his sons.

Trust in God
and you will
be strong.

"Judah, my middle son, is
a mighty warrior. Follow his
lead in battle."

When Mattathias died, Judah and his brothers crept back to Modin to bury him.

"We will continue what our father has begun," said Judah.

By now, Antiochus had heard about the rebel Jews. In a rage, he sent an army of 2,000 men to defeat them.

As Antiochus's army came sweating up a narrow hill road to Jerusalem, Judah and his men were ready for them. They pelted the soldiers with rocks and stones.

Antiochus's soldiers were thrown into confusion.

Those at the front tried to go back, but those at the back still pushed forward. Their battle formation was ruined, as the rows of soldiers became tangled together.

In the fierce fighting that followed, the king's general was killed. His shocked troops fled back down the hillside, where they were finished off by Judah's men.

"We've won!" cried Judah.

Word spread quickly about the amazing victory. As a sign of his strength, Judah became known as the Maccabee – the Hebrew word for hammer.

For eight days, Judah and his followers celebrated. "Every year at this time, Jews will hold an eight-day festival," Judah declared. "And we'll call it *Hanukkah*, meaning dedication, because today we dedicated our Temple to God once more."

Chapter 5

Festival of Lights

Over 2,000 years later, during
November or December
each year, Jews still
celebrate the festival
of Hanukkah.

Huge flames are lit in cities all over the world, in memory of the *menorah* that burned for eight days instead of one.

Hanukkah flames in Jerusalem, Israel.

And each night, as the sun goes down, Jewish families place a special candlestick, called a *hanukkiah*, on the table or in the window.

A boy lights a *hanukkiah* in a window. The idea behind this custom is for passers-by to see the lights and remember the miracle.

The *hanukkiah* is shaped like the Temple *menorah*. Wax candles are used, rather than oil, and the *hanukkiah* has eight main candles — one for each night of Hanukkah.

The ninth candle, the *shamash*, or servant candle, stands apart from the others. It is used to light the other candles.

A new candle is lit each night, until on the last night, all are burning.

On this *hanukkiah*, the *shamash* candle is raised above the others.

As the candles are lit, everyone says blessings in Hebrew or English. The blessings are followed by singing...

Oh Hanukkah, Oh Hanukkah,
come light the menorah,
Let's have a party, we'll all dance the hora.
Gather round the table, we'll give you a treat.
Dreidels to play with, latkes to eat.

And while we are playing,
The candles are burning low.
One for each night, they shed a sweet light,
To remind us of days long ago;
One for each night, they shed a sweet light,
To remind us of days long ago.

...and after that, the feasting begins.

40

A *sufganiyot*, a Hanukkah treat, dusted with sugar.

Most of the food is cooked in oil, as a reminder of the oil in the Temple *menorah*.

In Israel, everyone eats *sufganiyot* – delicious dough balls which are fried in oil and then topped with powdered sugar. They are sold in bakeries and from market stalls in the streets.

Jews from Eastern Europe fry potato pancakes, called *latkes*, which they eat with their Hanukkah meal.

Children play a special game at Hanukkah with a spinning top called a *dreidel* or *sevivon*. (Find out the rules on page 46.)

These are *dreidels*. They have Hebrew letters on their sides.

Some families give out Hanukkah presents, one for each night of Hanukkah, along with *gelt*, which are real or chocolate coins.

42

Today, Hanukkah is one of the most-loved Jewish festivals — especially by children. And as Jews gaze at the candlelight, they remember the freedom won by the Maccabees, and the importance for people everywhere to be able to worship their God in peace.

Latkes

Hanukkah *latkes* are one of the most popular Hanukkah foods, but they can be eaten all year round. Here's how they are made:

Ingredients

4 medium potatoes, peeled
1 medium onion, peeled
2 eggs, beaten
3 tablespoons of flour or breadcrumbs
Salt and pepper
Oil

1. The potatoes and onion are grated into a bowl. Then they are pressed down so that any liquid is squeezed out.

2. The eggs are mixed in.

3. The flour or breadcrumbs are added as well, until the mixture becomes doughy, but not too dry. Salt and pepper is sprinkled on too.

4. The mixture is shaped into thin patties.

5. About 1cm (¹/₂ inch) of oil is heated in a frying pan. The patties are fried in the oil, until the bottoms are golden brown. Then they are flipped over until both sides are golden brown.

6. The finished latkes are placed on a paper towel to drain, and eaten while they're still hot.

Some people sprinkle herbs onto their *latkes,* as you can see here.

Rules for playing dreidel

1. All the players are given an equal number of tokens. Each person then puts one token in the pot. The tokens can be coins, nuts or raisins.

2. Everyone takes turns to spin the *dreidel*. When the spinning stops, everyone looks at the Hebrew letter on top to see what happens.

NUN – Nothing happens – the next player takes a turn.

SHIN – The player must put one token into the pot.

HEY – The player can take half the tokens in the pot.

GIMEL – The player takes all the tokens in the pot.

3. When the pot is empty, everyone puts in one more token. The game finishes when one person wins all the tokens.

Hanukkah glossary

dreidel – a spinning top

hanukkiah – a nine-branch candlestick used to celebrate Hanukkah

Hebrew – the language of the Jewish people, still used in Israel today

menorah – the oil lamp in the Jewish *Temple*, with seven branches

sevivon – the *Hebrew* name for a spinning top

shamash – the central candle on the *hanukkiah* that is used to light all the other candles

Temple – a place of worship for the Jews

Internet links

For links to some fun websites about Hanukkah, go to the Usborne Quicklinks Website at **www.usborne-quicklinks.com** and type in the keywords **YR Hanukkah**.

Please note that Usborne Publishing cannot be responsible for any website other than its own.

A note on the Hanukkah story

Most Jewish festivals are found in the Bible. But the Bible had already been written by the time the Hanukkah story took place. Instead, the story is told in the *Books of the Maccabees*, which are found in a collection of writings called the *Apocrypha*. Hanukkah isn't a major festival, like Jewish New Year or Passover, but it is one of the most fun.

Series editor: Lesley Sims
Subject expert: Jan Roseman
Director of Education, Liberal Jewish Synagogue

ACKNOWLEDGEMENTS

Cover © Roy Morsch/CORBIS; pp6-7 © Z.Radovan/www.BibleLandPictures.com; pp36-37 © Gideon Mendel/CORBIS; p38 © David H. Wells/CORBIS; p39 © Jeff Spielman/The Image Bank/Getty Images; p41 © Brauner, Michael/StockFood; p42 (t) © John Wilkes Studio/Corbis, (b) © Lawrence Manning/Corbis; p43 © Sam Kittner/National Geographic/Getty Images; p45 © StockFood Creative/Getty Images.

First published in 2007 by Usborne Publishing Ltd., Usborne House, 83-85 Saffron Hill, London EC1N 8RT, England. www.usborne.com
Copyright © 2007 Usborne Publishing Ltd.